Redeeming All Things
Integral Mission and Creation Care

Rachel Mander

M-Series from im:press

Titles in print:

Corruption and the Church
by Martin Allaby

Living in God's Story
by Mark Galpin

Rethinking Church
by Johannes Reimer with Chris Wright

Rethinking Shame and Honour
by Arley Loewen

Integral Mission: Biblical Foundations
by Melba Maggay

Five Marks of Mission: making God's Mission ours
by Chris Wright

Redeeming All Things
Integral Mission and Creation Care
Rachel Mander

The M-series is a collection of short, accessible papers and articles from Micah Global, developed in response to the need for clear, authoritative statements on key themes. They form a foundation of historical and current ideas that contribute to our understanding and practice of integral mission. They aim to promote reflection, dialogue, articulation and action on the major concepts and issues that move us towards transforming mission.

The M-series is an essential resource for practitioners, theologians, students, leaders, and teachers.

Copyright Rachel Mander

The author asserts the moral right to be identified as the author of this work

Published 2022 by im:press - An imprint of Micah Global
www.micahglobal.org
ISBN: 978-1-4855-0010-0

All rights reserved.

No part of this book may be transmitted or reproduced in any form or by any means, including but not restricted to photocopying, recording, or by any information storage and retrieval system, without written permission from the publisher; except for brief quotations in printed reviews.

Printed and bound by Ingram Spark

Contents

Introduction	7
Creation Care: Integral to the gospel	11
Jesus: Creator and Redeemer	12
The Interdependence of Creation	14
What does it mean to proclaim the gospel?	20
Creation Care: Integral to Mission	21
Made to serve	21
Image-bearing is a missiological task	24
What does it mean to demonstrate the gospel?	28
The need for an integrated faith response now	33
A pressing and urgent crisis	33
We are the perpetrators of injustice	38
Lament	40
Urgent and Prophetic Ecological Responsibility	42
Conclusion	47
Bibliography and Further Reading	49

Introduction

I grew up in an independent evangelical church in Birmingham, UK; an upbringing for which I am very grateful. It's also an upbringing that left me completely bewildered when arriving at university and meeting fellow students at church who considered environmental care to be integral to their faith. In time, these students became friends whose conviction, and the commitments they had made as a result, challenged me to return to scripture and read it anew.

I can only tell you that this transformed my lived experience of my Christian faith and made it richer. This experience was a few years ago now, and I've since graduated, moved cities, and my conviction that caring for creation is part of God's mission has deepened.

Sometimes I am asked whether caring for creation is just the latest trend, particularly among those of my generation. I always reply that this isn't a new trend, but a rediscovery of something forgotten. As Christians we are called to bear witness to the love of God.

> God's love for this world in itself is greater than we dare imagine, and is a truth for all of time.

It's my hope that what follows in this booklet allows you to encounter God's love for this world anew.

This is the definition of integral mission from the Micah Global Declaration:

Integral mission or holistic transformation is the proclamation and demonstration of the gospel. It is not simply that evangelism and social involvement are to be done alongside each other. Rather, in integral mission our proclamation has social consequences as we call people to love and repentance in all areas of life. And our social involvement has evangelistic consequences as we bear witness to the transforming grace of Jesus Christ.

If we ignore the world, we betray the word of God which sends us out to serve the world. If we ignore the word of God, we have nothing to bring to the world. Justice and justification by faith, worship and political action, the spiritual and the material, personal change and structural change belong together. As in the life of Jesus, being, doing and saying are at the heart of our integral task.

> Creation care is a crucial part of the proclamation and demonstration of the gospel.

The Lausanne Global Consultation on Creation Care and the Gospel, convened in 2012, issued a Jamaica Call to Action. It asked for "the whole church, in dependence on the Holy Spirit, to respond radically and faithfully to care for God's creation, demonstrating our belief and hope in the transforming power of Christ." This call to action rejects the sidelining of creation care as 'secondary' to the gospel.

The church is situated within the context of our unsustainable consumption of the earth's abundance. The volume and extent of human activity - particularly that of industrialised nations - is causing environmental degradation and rising greenhouse gas emissions.

In the next couple of decades we will reach a global average temperature increase of 1.5 degrees from the pre-industrial baseline. After reaching 1.5 degrees, we are very likely to reach 2 degrees.

The 2018 Intergovernmental Panel on Climate Change (IPCC) quantifies the difference between 1.5 degrees and 2 degrees in this way:

> Limiting global warming to 1.5°C, compared with 2°C, could reduce the number of people both exposed to climate-related risks and susceptible to poverty by up to several hundred million by 2050.

That means within the next 30 years, several hundred million more people will be severely impacted by our failure to act now. Disadvantaged and vulnerable populations, some indigenous peoples, and local communities dependent on agricultural or coastal livelihoods are at "disproportionately higher risk of adverse consequences".

The church will be part of this context, responding to the far-reaching consequences for our health, livelihoods, food security, and water supply, as ecosystems struggle to adapt.

By 2100, we are likely to see warming of 2.6°C – 4.8°C.

At this rate of change, adult life for the young people in our churches will be radically different to our own. Crisis situations like those caused by the coronavirus pandemic will not be exceptions, they will be the norm.

Our current situation, and its projected consequences, give focus to the words of the Micah Declaration:

> If we ignore the world, we betray the word of God which sends us out to serve the world. If we ignore the word of God, we have nothing to bring to the world.

We are living in a way which outstrips the replenishment of the vital systems on which all life depends. Climate change, pollution, and biodiversity and habitat loss are all outworkings of these choices. As the church we must defend the life God has made, and become a living example of God's reconciled world.

The church is part of creation, connected inextricably, it cannot be ignored. This is what integral mission and creation care is all about.

Creation Care: Integral to the gospel

Creation care is a crucial part of the proclamation and demonstration of the gospel. In the words of John Stott, "The gospel itself includes God's creation as well as his work of redemption".

This chapter examines the place of creation care in the proclamation of the gospel. The gospel is good news, and it is good news for us. However, we distort and reduce it if we stop here, thinking that people are its only focus. Our understanding of the gospel needs to acknowledge that just as there is no gospel without God, there is no gospel without the rest of creation.

> Once we see that the gospel centres on God's own purposes, and that those purposes are for the restoration and reconciliation of all creation, it follows that there is no gospel without care for the rest of creation. There is no gospel without creation care.

What does creation care mean then? It means loving creation as God does, leading to attitudes and actions that encourage the flourishing of the earth and all God has made.

> As image-bearers of God, we should **respect non-human creation**, treating our fellow creatures with **neighbourly love**.

Jesus: Creator and Redeemer

Before we proclaim the gospel we must first reflect on what the gospel is. Jesus, in his ministry, proclaims the gospel of the Kingdom of God: the reign of God over all.

As NT Wright explains,

> There are a thousand different ways of describing the good news—the Gospel—but the shortest way is the one Jesus Himself announced: "The time is fulfilled and the Kingdom of God is arriving" (Mark 1:15). In other words, it's all about how God became King. It's about the actual inauguration of God's Kingdom on earth as in heaven.

The gospel is fundamentally about God's rule. To accept the gospel, we must recognise the one who *reigns*. As Christians, we affirm this is Jesus. Jesus is King, the one who reigns. We are people who affirm the Lordship of Jesus Christ.

Who is Jesus, the one who reigns? The bible tells us Jesus is both the Creator and the Redeemer.

---

15 The Son is the image of the invisible God, the firstborn over all creation. 16 For in him all things were created: things in heaven and on earth, visible and invisible, whether thrones or powers or rulers or authorities; all things have been created through him and for him. 17 He is before all things, and in him all things hold together. 18 And he is the head of the body, the church; he is the beginning and the firstborn from among the dead, so that in everything he might have the supremacy.

19 For God was pleased to have all his fullness dwell in him, 20 and through him to reconcile to himself all things, whether things on earth or things in heaven, by making peace through his blood, shed on the cross.

Colossians 1:15-20

Jesus is the Creator; the firstborn over all creation, all things have been created through him and for him. Jesus is also the Redeemer; the firstborn from among the dead, who repays, recovers and saves all things. Jesus, through his blood, reconciles all things to himself whether things on earth or things in heaven.

It is clear from this passage that Jesus is Creator and Redeemer of "all things". All creation is through him, for him, and reconciled in him.

What does this mean for Christians, who affirm the Lordship of Jesus Christ?

Firstly, it means we believe the good news that the reign of God applies to all creation.

> As the Creator of all things, Jesus' kingdom has always included all of creation.

As the Redeemer of all things, Jesus' kingdom always will include all creation. And yet, how often do we think about Jesus' relationship with non-human creation?

Secondly, it means accepting Jesus' Lordship changes our understanding of the whole world. When accepting Jesus, we also accept God's purposes for creation above our own purposes for creation, and therefore we act in accordance with a new understanding of our own place within all God has made (see more about this in Chapter 2).

This makes creation care part of our recognition that Jesus Christ is Lord.

The 2010 Cape Town Commitment puts it this way:

> ...to proclaim the gospel that says Jesus is Lord is to proclaim the gospel that includes the earth, since Christ's Lordship is over all creation. Creation care is thus a gospel issue within the Lordship of Jesus Christ (CTC I.7.A).

The doctrine of creation holds together with the doctrine of redemption. As Kenyan theologian Samson Gitau says, "There can be no redemption without creation".

The Interdependence of Creation

Redemption is the reconciliation of all creation - whether things on earth or things in heaven - under the reign of God. Or in other words: 'the kingdom of God is creation healed'.

> The narrative arc of scripture is consistent. It always presents a vision of interdependent flourishing as the continuous intention, and ultimate end of God's creation.

The biblical narrative begins with God and the story of creation.

God - Father, Son, and Holy Spirit - is communal and relational. The relationship between the Godhead is one of continual movement of mutuality, reciprocity and communion. (This relationship is described by the Greek term *perichoresis*).

As God is communal and relational, so too is creation. Creation shares in community and relationship. Richard Bauckham captures this in his description of the 'community of creation':

> All God's creatures are first and foremost creatures, ourselves included. All earthly creatures share the same Earth; and all participate in an interrelated and interdependent community, orientated above all to God our common Creator.

Genesis upholds the independent value of each part of creation. This is expressed in the refrain "and it was good". Creation is also designed as an interdependent whole. The change to the refrain at the end of the sixth day reflects this: "God looked at all that he had made, and it was all very good" (Genesis 1:31). This declaration applies to all God has made, biodiversity and ecosystems, as well as humanity.

The earth is part of the community to which we belong, and into which God created us. This understanding continues through scripture. The Psalms tell how the majesty, order, power and beauty of creation proclaim God's character, and invite us to join creation's worship of her Creator. God continues to sustain and renew the earth, taking delight in even those creatures that are mysterious and dangerous to humanity (Job 38-41), and providing breath, food, and habitats to all living creatures (Psalm 104).

One way of understanding creation's interdependence is to think of God's creation as a triangle of relationships. Creation establishes life-giving relationships between God, humanity, and the earth. This is also mirrored in the triangle of relationships in the Hebrew Bible, between God–Israel–the land.

It is this set of relationships that fractures when sin enters. Our brokenness extends beyond God's relationship with humanity, which is visible when Adam and Eve hide from God. The humanity-Earth relationship fractures when God expels Adam and Eve from the garden. Finally, the relationship between God and the Earth breaks ("Cursed is the ground." Genesis 3:17).

And yet, a few chapters on, God makes explicit his intention to restore the interdependent flourishing of creation. In Genesis 9, God makes a covenant with Noah and all creation. This covenant establishes the future of the earth as a reliable place where God will work out his purposes to rescue all things (Genesis 8:18-21). There is no requirement placed on Noah or the other creatures: God states the promise and signs it with a rainbow (Genesis 9:12-17).

In Exodus, God makes another covenant with Israel. God desires to show himself to all nations by making Israel into a kingdom of priests who will represent his character (Exodus 1-15). God rescues Israel from slavery in Egypt and promises to dwell in their midst and bring them into the land promised to Abraham (Exodus 3:7-20). Israel, in return, is asked to obey the terms of the covenant embodied in the laws given by God at Mt. Sinai, including the Ten Commandments (Exodus 20-23).

It is significant that both these covenants involve wider creation. In Genesis 9, animate creatures are partners in the covenant and God's promise concerns the future of the earth. In the covenant with Israel, God's promise concerns the people's connection with the land.

Case Study: The Philippines

The Philippines is a low-lying nation of over 7,000 islands dominated by coastal communities. It is also highly susceptible to extreme weather events and increasing urbanisation is posing a significant challenge for sustainable development.

In 2013, Typhoon Haiyan struck, at the time the most powerful typhoon ever recorded to hit land. Climate change is known to have increased the severity of this storm. The Eastern Visayas like Samar and Leyte islands were the most affected in the country.

Jasmine Kwong, a Creation Care Advocate working with OMF, says that even now communities are still recovering. After Typhoon Haiyan, many lost their livelihoods. Fishermen lost their boats. Coconut farmers lost their trees. But since these communities live along the sea, the easiest option for most was to return to fishing. The increased competition has affected fish harvests as well as overall fish stocks. In this way...

> Caring for creation is an integral part of seeking the well-being of entire communities and places.

For this reason, creation care often requires addressing the deeper causes of environmental issues. In the urban context of the Philippines, one challenge is the high prevalence and use of single-use sachets (e.g. shampoo, soya sauce, chips, toothpaste). Many of the urban poor cannot afford to buy more than the smallest quantity of goods because they are daily wage earners with no savings. To meet the demand of millions of Filipinos in this situation, big companies readily produce millions of single-use sachets. These little sachets, when not properly disposed of, end up blocking the drainage systems in Manila during rainstorms. This causes major flooding, particularly in urban poor areas. The biggest problem is not the purchase of the sachets, but the poverty and inequality which underlie it.

Jasmine says, "The issues are entrenched and can feel overwhelming, but something I'm learning, what excites and grounds me, is seeing how God uses people wherever they are planted and knowing that it is God alone who ultimately saves the planet".

A number of local groups across different regions are responding to these issues. One social enterprise on Negros Island is helping to facilitate a 'circular economy' by providing people with alternatives to the single-use sachets. Customers are given goods in containers from their local sari-sari (small convenience store) which are returned and reused. Another NGO in Camarines Sur is training young adults in marine conservation education and coral reef restoration, ensuring sustainable fishing is a community effort.

> "There's no separation between the secular and the sacred; it's all sacred if you're following Jesus.

It's wonderful to see people make this realisation. Alongside dedicated projects which address some of the structural aspects of creation care, we have a responsibility and opportunity to embed creation care into our lives in whatever our own context happens to be, as a response to Jesus, and as a way of connecting with God in the places we live.

Last year, we started an instagram account "omf.creationcare" where we profile stories of Christians who are responding to this realisation:

an interior designer who talks with clients about mindful consumption, a clothing designer who repurposes textile waste, a pastor who is also a bird photographer or another pastor who started composting on his balcony.

God uses us wherever we are planted.

In scripture, the context for humanity's relationship with God is always the earth.

This is why Brueggemann regards land to be a central theme of biblical faith. He says of the people of Israel that they "never had a desire for a relation with Yahweh in a vacuum, but only in land".

The New Covenant ushered in by Jesus' crucifixion and resurrection extends these themes. Once more, the covenant involves the wider creation. Jesus' death on the cross is a triumph over all death: human death, but also the forms of death experienced by the rest of creation. Once more, God establishes the earth as the context for humanity's relationship with God. Jesus' resurrected body is our model for the promise of life in the new creation. Bodily resurrection, on a resurrected earth.

This is where the biblical narrative ends, with God and the promise of the "new creation".

The ultimate end of God's creation is a vision of interdependent flourishing. Creation restored: God-Humanity-Earth realising *shalom* (a Hebrew word often translated as 'peace'). God's vision is a unity and wholeness throughout all creation.

What does it mean to proclaim the gospel?

As people, a part of an interdependent creation, God calls us to proclaim and demonstrate the gospel. This gospel is the Lordship of Jesus Christ, who is the Creator and Redeemer of all creation. Jesus' Lordship means recognising ultimate authority and worth is found in Jesus. To proclaim the gospel is to proclaim Jesus' everlasting reign over everything, both the heavens and the earth.

As Christians, accepting Jesus' Lordship, we thereby accept the purposes God has for creation of interdependent flourishing. We accept our own right place within the creation Jesus has made. This is a true humanity which acknowledges that, in the words of Kathryn Greene-McCreight, "there is no true humanity without other creatures of God".

> In a profound sense, our flourishing as people depends on the flourishing of the earth.

In the next chapter we explore the role of people within the creation of God.

Creation Care: Integral to Mission

To accept Jesus' Lordship is to accept the purposes God has for creation and to accept our place within creation. To proclaim the gospel is to proclaim Jesus' everlasting reign over everything, both the heavens and the earth. To demonstrate the gospel is to be the image of (to witness to and embody) God in creation, following Christ who defines the image of God for us.

How should we understand our place in creation, and, consequently, the integral role of creation care in our mission?

Made to serve

> Then God said, 'Let us make humankind in our image, in our likeness, so that they may rule over the fish in the sea and the birds in the sky, over the livestock and all the wild animals, and over all the creatures that move along the ground.'
>
> Genesis 1:26

God makes people to rule. But what is the character of this rule?

It is sometimes argued that the role God gives people in terms of 'rule' means we are 'set apart' from the rest of creation, and given ultimate authority over other creatures. This connects with ideas of human 'dominion' as domination, submitting creation to human interests and ends.

This approach, and others like it, leads to an anthropocentric worldview which privileges humanity at the expense of nature's exploitation.

However, we should look again. This verse says people are made in the image and likeness of God "so that they may rule". This gives us a very different understanding of the character of ruling, because scripture tells us the intent of our rule should be to image God.

Indeed, the real meaning of 'dominion' in Genesis 1 is 'lordship'. This is not the lordship of totalitarian rulers, at the top of a creaturely hierarchy. Rather, as Sarah Ann Sharkey recognises, the word for dominion (*rada*) is associated with the biblical concept of royal rule, where the king rules by serving the people and the land, ensuring that they both flourish.

Jesus is our perfect model both of lordship and imaging God. It is Christ who defines for us the image of God. What do we find when we look to Christ to understand what it is to image God and rule in his creation? In the words of Jonathan Moo:

> "We discover one who was in the very form of God and yet did not take advantage of what was rightfully his, humbling himself in the form of a servant and going to death on a cross… Our rule as God's image bearers then, finds its model in the self-sacrificial love of God displayed in Christ."

Human dominion over the earth can only be exercised in the light of Jesus' command that the greatest is the one who serves (Luke 22.26). We image God in enabling all creation to flourish.

In Genesis, we are entrusted to lead from amongst creation, reflecting God's character and purposes for all creation. As people we are not 'apart from' but 'a part of' creation. Being made 'in the image and likeness of God' conveys both privilege and great responsibility. God creates people to reflect his loving, sustaining character towards the earth and its creatures.

'Dominion', then, is not understood as 'domination'; our actions towards the other creatures God has made must be consistent with the biblical affirmation that all creation exists for the glory of God.

Creation displays God's splendour. In our actions we can honour the flourishing and fruitfulness of creation and, therefore, also honour God. Instead, we often choose to diminish creation through our greed and self-centeredness.

> When we destroy, pollute, and drive species to extinction, we surely dishonour God.

Our systems of industry, technology, agriculture, deforestation and pollution are undertaken without reference to the processes of nature. We think we can reshape the world. Over the last 50 years, it is estimated that humans have changed ecosystems more, and faster, than any time in human history. But taking seriously the role given to us by God means that the character of our rule is service. John Stott says: "In exercising our God-given dominion, we are not creating the processes of nature, but cooperating with them."

This emphasis on cooperating with the processes of nature is supported by the second chapter of Genesis that contains a parallel account of creation, adding detail to the narrative of the first chapter.

> Then the LORD God took the man and put him in the garden of Eden to tend [dress, KJV] and keep it.
>
> Genesis 2:15

Tend (Hebrew *abad*) means 'to work or serve'. In the context of the garden, it refers to cultivation. The reason the KJV translates this word as 'dress' is that it has the nuance of adornment, embellishment, and improvement. Likewise, 'keep' (Hebrew *shamar*) means 'to exercise great care over'.

God therefore expresses a wish that people act as caretakers. A caretaker maintains and protects his or her land so they can return it to its owner, in as good or better condition than when they received it. The vocation of Adam and Eve is one of cultivation.

Image-bearing is a missiological task

Our right place in creation is one which enables all life to flourish.

Reflecting God in caring for creation is fundamental to who we are: "It is our first great commission and our clear job description."

How does this job description relate to mission? At this point it is helpful to examine what we mean by mission. In the words of Chris Wright, our mission:

> "... means our committed participation as God's people, at God's invitation and command, in God's own mission within the history of God's world for the redemption of God's creation."

It is easy to think of mission in anthropocentric terms. Doing so has been part of the reason many Christians have emphasised the primacy of evangelism, on the understanding that evangelism addresses the greatest human need. And yet, while there is truth in this, as Chris Wright emphasises, our mission is a participation in God's purposes, which are for all creation.

This is reflected by the understanding of mission found in The Cape Town Commitment,

"Integral mission means discerning, proclaiming, and living out, the biblical truth that the gospel is God's good news, through the cross and resurrection of Jesus Christ, for individual persons, and for society, and for creation. All three are broken and suffering because of sin; all three are included in the redeeming love and mission of God; all three must be part of the comprehensive mission of God's people."

From the start of Genesis, as we have seen in this chapter, God invites us into mission. The mission we are invited into is a committed participation which enables all creation to flourish.

Case Study: Sikkim and North Bengal, India

Abhay Pradhan is part of Mission Himalaya, an indigenous church planting organisation.

In 2017, Abhay attended training on Integral Mission and Creation Care organised by EFICOR. He explains, "This training helped me so much and challenged me to do something. After I returned back from the training, Mission Himalaya started training churches on the biblical basis for Creation Care. Brother Mang from EFICOR Delhi also came to facilitate a series of training across North Bengal and Sikkim region. Leaders were excited by the training and they went back with action steps on Creation Care to be executed in their respective areas."

In 2018, Mission Himalaya mobilised an initiative called Himalayan Plantation Week from 5th-12th June, with an intention to challenge Himalayan laity to plant a tree. Churches responded positively; Himalayan Environment Week was observed in more than twenty places by around forty churches and Christian organisations. It has been an annual event since then. In 2019 a collaborative initiative called CT Gen or 'Caretakers Generation' was started. The main vision of the movement is to raise a generation of Caretakers who would express the love for the creator by taking care of God's creation.

"Caring for creation has impacted every aspect of my life. My wife and I made changes to how we deal with our own waste and had conversations with our neighbours about this too. It has become a vital part of our family life. Some of the impacts have been surprising! One of my friends who had a bad experience with Christianity saw Christianity in a different light when I shared with him about caring for creation. He has been supportive of my work though he is not a Christian, and he has recently started a business based on the circular economy, which he said was partly inspired by my passion for creation care."

"I definitely see God's creativity and sense of humour in creation. I am hopeful for the church to own the vision of creation care and reflect the goodness of God to their neighbours. Too often we have failed to realise this. A couple of years back I was travelling by bus to Gangtok and sitting next to me was a monk. We exchanged greetings and started talking about life. I asked him about Buddhism and asked him to tell me what he liked and did not like about Christianity. He said that he had seen people's lives changed in Christianity and that was a good thing. The thing he did not like, he said, was the fact that we Christians do not value nature at all. I shared with him about God who loved His creation and commanded man to take care of the creation and how we were learning to obey God and things we were doing. So, you see how the world is viewing the church? We as a church have not been able to reflect God's goodness to the world."

"Caring for creation is part of our calling as Christians. The church has been bestowed with immense power to transform and bring God's kingdom and *shalom*, I hope we can take this seriously."

The great commission in the New Testament continues this call. The instruction of Jesus in Matthew 28 starts with a declaration of his lordship ("All authority in heaven and on earth has been given to me." Matthew 28:18), in recognition that our mission always starts with God, and derives only from the purposes of God for all creation. Neither is the mission God gives us in the New Testament anthropocentric; the great commission in Mark 16 states, "Go into all the world and preach the gospel to all creation."

What does it mean to demonstrate the gospel?

Our mission means upholding the life God has made, demonstrating the gospel by becoming a living example of God's reconciled world. Participating in God's mission means in part that "we ought to live in a way that is consistent with creation's eventual freedom from futility and ruin when all things are made new."

As we accept our part in creation, we accept as our guide the gentle and just servant-hearted leadership exemplified by Jesus Christ.

> Too often we seek from creation what is best for ourselves.

Instead, we should seek the best for creation in keeping with God's care for us and the rest of creation, which is marked "by tenderness, compassion, mercy, and ultimately sacrifice".

How much of our activity - even the so-called traditional forms of church 'missional activity' - reflects creation's eventual freedom? To what extent can we say our treatment of creation reflects the character of God's care for us? It is likely far less than many of us would be willing to admit. The destruction and exploitation of creation for our own benefit is a pervasive part of our present-day context, even within the church.

Case Study: 'Vida Abundante', Peru

Peru has weak environmental policy. Small farm owners gain little or no support from the government and there is a serious lack of commitment from authorities when it comes to promoting sustainable agriculture. There is also a lack of environmental awareness amongst church communities, across all denominations and at every level of leadership; This extends to the national curriculum, there is no teaching about sustainable environmental practices or the effects of climate change.

Pilar Vicentelo has found her ministry working to change this. "At university, I came to understand my path in life was to be linked with God's creation. I understood that my life has purpose because I am created by God and part of God's creation."

Pilar started working at 'Vida Abundante' (Abundant Life) in 2007 when the organisation was first set-up. Vida Abundante aims to develop sustainable living practices through different projects, working very closely with children in primary education, "the future of the country". "Our work is possibly the only way that some children will come into contact with the knowledge and skills they will need to become environmentally responsible citizens."

"We have various projects, including introducing vegetable gardens in schools. We see children learn to love plants and their environment, and to feel relaxed in it. We work with a number of children who are from highly vulnerable families, so it is so important to not only help them gain head knowledge, but also to help them rest and have confidence in themselves.

As an organisation we know that 'if people see creation, they can't say that they don't know God.'

I have learned how closely linked God is to his creation and how important it is to have a fruitful relationship with God's creation, as well as with the Creator himself. The abundant life that Jesus gave us means that we should take care of the abundance of life that is all around us. The opportunities God gives us to know Him are very diverse and very creative."

"We need to read the word of God with a more open mind and a clean, clear spirit of obedience. The scriptures tell us of the responsibility that we have to care for creation, and we can't escape this. We need to wake up from being passive and inactive. Christians are part of destructive environmental practices. This needs to change."

We should consider again the interdependence of creation. Our flourishing as people depends on the flourishing of the earth. As Craig Sorley says, "when creation groans, people groan".

This is something being made particularly evident by the challenges we face at present. Grace Ji-Sun Kim and Hilda Koster put it this way; "theology and doctrine have focused on humanity and made the 'rest of creation' external to the story of God with human beings. Climate change brings home that there is no such externality."

This interdependence is being increasingly recognised. The UN Sustainable Development Goals (SDGs) were adopted by all UN member states in 2015. The 17 SDGs define an integrated approach to human development and environmental sustainability and succeed the earlier Millennium Development Goals. These goals recognise the importance of caring for creation both implicitly and explicitly: a sustainable environment is essential in tackling poverty, achieving food security, and health and well-being (SDGs 1-3), but the goals also include tackling climate change and conserving and restoring marine and terrestrial ecosystems (SDGs 13-15). In fact, analysis of the 169 targets underlying the goals considers environmental resilience and sustainability and a transformed understanding of the relationship between humanity and the natural world to be essential to their achievement.

This shouldn't come as a surprise. In the words of Dr. Stella Simiyu, a Kenyan biologist and advisor to both A Rocha and IUCN (International Union for Nature Conservation):

"The rural poor depend directly on the natural resource base. This is where their pharmacy is, this is where their supermarket is, this is in fact their fuel station, their power company, their water company. What would happen to you if these things were removed from your local neighbourhood? Therefore, we really cannot afford not to invest in environmental conservation."

The church is a place of reorientation. We orient ourselves towards Jesus Christ and use our lives to demonstrate the gospel which proclaims his reign.

This demonstration is crucial. If we proclaim that Jesus Christ is Lord, who is Creator and Redeemer of all things, but beyond our church walls we destroy and devalue what we believe is his, then we either do not truly believe Jesus is Lord, or we are a church of hypocrites.

Our reorientation towards Jesus requires our Christ-like care for all creation.

Caring for creation, for Jesus' sake, is costly. When our societies value convenience and comfort to the detriment of the rest of creation, making decisions that avoid the exploitation of the environment can feel burdensome. However, as the church, we believe the gospel brings life, and we are prepared to pay the cost of proclaiming and demonstrating this gospel.

Our care for creation is a witness to Jesus, who redeems lives, and the Holy Spirit, who we confess in the Nicene Creed as the Lord and the Giver of Life. As we live under the rule of God and contribute to the flourishing of the earth, we also contribute to the flourishing of all people, and demonstrate the gospel.

Considering what the demonstration of the gospel looks like in the present-day context of the church is the subject of the next chapter.

The need for an integrated faith response now

At the Lausanne Global Consultation on Creation Care and the Gospel, convened in 2012, a Call to Action was issued, premised on two major convictions. Firstly, that creation care is indeed a "gospel issue within the lordship of Christ". And secondly, that we face a crisis which is pressing, urgent, and that must be resolved in our generation, one which requires "urgent and prophetic ecological responsibility" (CTC I.7.A).

The first of these convictions has been explored in the previous chapters. The second conviction is the focus of this chapter: what is the crisis we are faced with, and what does it mean to respond with an urgent and prophetic ecological responsibility?

A pressing and urgent crisis

> When was the last time you thought about how you access water?

Stop for a moment, and allow yourself to think about what would happen, and how you would feel, if your usual sources of water were no longer available, or your access to them was restricted.

Back in February 2018, the head of Cape Town's disaster operations centre was working on plans to cope with millions of people simultaneously experiencing this very scenario. Cape Town was preparing for so-called Day Zero, when the water in the city's reservoirs would hit lows of 13.5% of capacity, and engineers would turn off the water supply for millions of homes.

In the end, strict rationing and careful planning eventually alleviated the crisis. However, droughts like the one Cape Town faced are becoming more frequent and more severe.

Environmental degradation is increasing water-stress globally. Climate change is bringing droughts and heatwaves across the globe, as well as floods and sea level rises. Pollution is increasing, both of freshwater supplies and underground aquifers; depletion of those aquifers can also make the remaining water more saline. Fertilisers leaching nitrates into the supplies can make water unsuitable for drinking or irrigation.

By 2025, it is estimated that half the world's population will be living in water-stressed areas.

The planning for Day Zero contended with major risks: water shortages, sanitation failures, disease outbreaks and conflict due to competition for scarce resources. This is illustrative of an important concept; climate change and other forms of environmental degradation amplify existing risks of social and economic disruption. In particular, they exacerbate migration, conflict, and inequality. For this reason, climate change is known as a 'threat multiplier'.

The example here is water scarcity. But water scarcity is far from the only example. We face a multi-dimensional environmental crisis with far-reaching impacts. Extreme weather events of increasingly great magnitudes are causing more devastation, food systems are under strain as crops fail to adapt to changing seasons, and biodiversity loss reduces the resilience of ecosystems and contributes to species extinction.

> It is difficult to fully grasp the extent and urgency of what we are facing.

Human activity is directly killing an increasing number of plants and animals and accelerating the extinction rate of species. This loss of biodiversity has reached critical levels, threatening the collapse of entire ecosystems. The Earth is undergoing the sixth mass extinction in its history. Up to 58,000 species are believed to be lost each year. Vertebrate populations declined by 60% between 1970–2014. Loss of vertebrate populations in some countries exceeds 85%, while freshwater vertebrate populations have declined by 83% across the world. At the current rates, insects could be extinct within a century.

Case Study: Atewa Forest, Ghana

The Atewa Forest is a mountain forest, one of the most biodiverse in West Africa. It is also the source of three major rivers, which provide water for over five million people.

The forest faces a number of threats including illegal logging, farm encroachment and the hunting of animals. All of these activities undermine the capacity of the forest to absorb and filter rainwater. Small-scale mining also pollutes the rivers, as toxic metals make the water unsuitable for consumption. Some water treatment plants have had to close because the water is so polluted it cannot be treated.

However, the biggest threat to the forest is from large-scale commercial bauxite mining (the ore of aluminium). The hills of the forest hold deposits of bauxite and many international companies are vying to exploit this through open cast mining. The Ghanaian government is currently under pressure to accept offers from China to begin extraction.

Seth Appiah-Kubi, National Director of A Rocha Ghana, says "Creation is for our Father, and as children of God we are proud of God's creation. It would be a failure on our part to stand by and watch our heritage be destroyed. You can't destroy such a place".

A Rocha Ghana is fronting an international campaign against the mining taking place. Mining will harm or destroy increasingly fragile ecosystems, contribute to the extinction of threatened species, and directly impact local communities whose livelihoods depend on the river.

Seth says, "Central to all this is our faith. We were never made to be a campaigning organisation, and we don't take it lightly, but we cannot just be quiet".

Ghana experienced a 60% rise in primary forest loss between 2008 and 2017 - the highest rise in any tropical country, according to the U.S.-based Global Forest Watch, with trees lost to illegal (and legal) mining, logging and expanding cocoa farms.

In December 2019 the Government of Ghana released a map showing the extent of the exploratory drilling that they have been undertaking in Atewa forest, which is far more extensive than feared. The drilling accounts for a large percentage of the forested area above 750m altitude, a critical area for biodiversity.

Seth continues, "I'm a trained accountant. This all started with a few friends when we started questioning why the church was not active. In 1999 we set up Eden Conservation Society which then became part of the A Rocha family in 2003. We now contribute to national policies, engaging at all levels. We do what we can."

"We're confronted with a gloomy outlook, but we're excited always to make progress, and although it is not always good news, we are strengthened together."

In July 2020, A Rocha Ghana filed a case against the government.

"Creation itself is looking to Christ for redemption, that's what motivates us."

Biodiversity and climate change are connected. Biodiversity loss can make ecosystems less effective at absorbing carbon dioxide, worsening climate change. Climate change can cause species extinction as rising global temperatures alter the conditions species are suited for, worsening biodiversity loss.

In the next couple of decades, we will reach a global average temperature increase of 1.5 degrees from the pre-industrial baseline. By 2100, we are likely to see warming of 2.6°C – 4.8°C.

As the global average temperature increases, we enter even further into a domain of risk. We could find ourselves perpetually overwhelming our emergency systems, as has happened in situations of crisis during the coronavirus pandemic.

Indeed, the experiences of 2020 (and 2021) should lead us to take our situation very seriously. Pandemics like Covid-19 and environmental crises interlink. They are both caused by the widespread destruction of ecosystems.

Our management of the coronavirus pandemic has caused extensive suffering and death. But pandemics and climate risk share many of the same attributes. Both stem from the human misuse and lack of careful guardianship of the natural world. Both affect systems, causing their direct impacts and knock-on effects to multiply fast across an interconnected world. Both have nonlinear socioeconomic impacts which grow disproportionately once they breach certain thresholds (such as hospital capacity to treat pandemic patients). Finally - tragically - they both disproportionately affect the most vulnerable.

We are the perpetrators of injustice

We are failing to care for creation, and consequently, our neighbours.

In the words of Jonathan Moo, we are called to live "as instantiations of the kingdom of God, members of a resistance movement against all that would destroy God's creation". And yet, in many ways the church is complicit in the crises of climate change and environmental degradation. How many people would look around them and characterise the church as a resistance movement against all that would destroy God's creation?

We are the perpetrators of injustice.

We are unjust in our greed. In our exploitation of creation, and in our actions which lead to species extinction.

> God committed the care of creation to us, but we have been careless.

(Jeremiah 2:7). God's concern extends to every living thing. Even if we were not harming other people in our actions, we would be guilty of injustice. In the light of today's collapse in biodiversity we need to read anew the biblical account of God's saving work at the time of Noah. Here we see that God's desire is not only to rescue humans but to ensure that every species should be kept alive upon the earth (Genesis 7:3), and God's covenant which follows the flood is repeatedly affirmed as including every living creature and the earth itself (Genesis 9:8-17). In practice, biodiversity loss inevitably affects the poorest first and worst, but even were this not so, our missional calling – like Noah's – includes biodiversity conservation.

We are unjust in our production systems. Production in the poorest countries is disproportionately for the benefit of consumers in the wealthiest. It is the wealthy who consume the most fossil fuels, and yet it is the poor who live with the consequences of the environmental degradation caused by their extraction. The profits of extracting fossil fuels in the poorest countries are reported by companies registered in the wealthiest. The headquarters of major oil companies such as, Shell (The Netherlands/UK), BP (UK), Total SA (France), Saudi Aramco (Saudi Arabia), Exxon Mobil (US), and Sinopec Group (China) are often thousands of miles away from the countries and communities affected by their oil extraction. The list of countries most affected by climate change and environmental degradation looks very different.

We are unjust in our consumption; guilty of ecologically unequal exchange. The wealthiest countries are responsible, both historically and presently, for the majority of greenhouse gas emissions; the top 10% of the global population by income are responsible for half of global emissions.

We are unjust in our mismanagement of present impacts, in our inaction, and in our failure to reimagine the status quo. The environmental crises we face have a disproportionate impact on vulnerable populations who are least responsible, are least economically resourced to be able to adapt and are least involved in global decision-making. Islands such as Tuvalu, the Solomon Islands, the Maldives, Kiribati and Fiji will no longer exist by the end of the century, but the people who live there do not have the power to make other countries change their trajectory. While others suffer, we remain reluctant to really change.

We are unjust in the future choices we are foreclosing.

It is as Nazmul Chowdhury, a development expert from Bangladesh, says - "Forget making poverty history. Climate change will make poverty permanent." We are limiting the choices of future generations and exacerbating inequality, and we do this while knowing our consumption patterns now have potentially catastrophic outcomes for generations of people who will lose their livelihoods or their lives in a destabilised climate.

Lament

Let's return to the challenge at the end of Chapter 2.

If we proclaim that Jesus Christ is Lord, who is Creator of Redeemer of all things, but beyond our church walls we destroy and devalue what we believe is his, then we either do not truly believe Jesus is Lord, or we are a church of hypocrites.

When we read afresh of the injustice we perpetrate and are complicit to, we should recognise ourselves as hypocrites.

> Our response to this should first be lament.

Lament means grieving death and destruction in all its forms, recognising that the world has departed from the purposes God has for what he has made, and we are complicit in this departure. It is an expression of faith. Holding our pain before God, lament confesses that grief over loss and belief in God's saving help are part of the same reality. Lament is modelled to us in the psalms in the context of worship.

Lament also prevents us from becoming escapist. It stops us averting our eyes at the sight of death, or constructing our lives in ways which allow us to pretend we are not part of the suffering of others.

Grief is a vitally important part of theology. David Atkinson puts this best:

> We need a theology that is more robust than the optimistic wish that everything will work out all right.

"We need a theology that is more robust than the optimistic wish that everything will work out all right. We need a theology that hears the words of judgement the eighth-century BC prophets spoke to God's people when they had abandoned God's ways, and given in to injustice. A theology that recognises that if we continue in the way of sinfulness, stupidity, overconsumption, 'extractivism' and greed, we most likely, and a future generation most certainly, are destined for some catastrophe. A theology that can address the strategies of denial among politicians and those who wield corporate power. A theology that may take us by way of Gethsemane and the cross before we reach Easter, by way of grief and mourning and repentant change, before we celebrate hope."

In this way, lament is a recognition that the world has departed from the purposes God has for what he has made. In our love for God and all he has made, we grieve.

Lament does not mean that we do not have hope.

After all, at the grave of Lazarus, Jesus wept. Even for one who would be raised again.

Instead, lament is connected with love. At the grave of Lazarus in John 11, the Jews, seeing Jesus' grief, remarked 'See how he loved him!'

If we love creation as God does, we will surely lament its destruction.

The same love that moves us to lament should lead us into repentance.

Urgent and Prophetic Ecological Responsibility

Lament also helps us to reckon with our injustice, in readiness for repentance. We can repent only when we refuse to push blame elsewhere, when we acknowledge where we are and where we must turn. We must ask: "We want God's justice. Whose justice is that?"

At that point, lament leads to the change required by repentance.

Repentance means to 'turn from'. Logically, repentance must be embodied in action, as Archbishop Thabo Makgoba says: "Words, words and more words will not reverse environmental degradation or carbon emissions, but our actions together can."

How should we change? What does it mean to live as instantiations of the kingdom of God, members of a resistance movement against all that would destroy God's creation? To demonstrate 'urgent and prophetic ecological responsibility'?

A good starting place is to go back to our understanding of integral mission:

> If we ignore the world, we betray the word of God which sends us out to serve the world. If we ignore the word of God, we have nothing to bring to the world.

Our starting place must be God, the redemption of Christ, and the transforming power of the Spirit.

If our response to the crisis we face is to add on some bullet points of creation care activities to our list of what constitutes 'mission', we will have missed the point.

Creation care derives from our response to the Creator, the Lordship of Jesus, and in this sense – when practised properly – it is no less than partnering with God in the reconciliation of all things.

Case Study: Bonn, Germany

Bonn is home to the World Evangelical Alliance Sustainability Center (WEASC) established in 2018, a strategic 'UN city'. It connects the world's 600 million evangelical Christians with global efforts to achieve the United Nations Sustainable Development Goals (SDGs) and equips and connects evangelical church communities to care for creation.

One example of the work they are engaged in is their Project 20'25. This initiative works towards a commitment to assist 20% of the global evangelical footprint, including educational institutions, medical facilities, churches, households and other affiliated entities, to transition to renewable energy by 2025.

Matthias K. Boehning is the Director of WEASC. "We have such a full gospel running from creation to redemption, and relevant to the world."

> People are asking how they can live with meaning.

"As the church, we need to take our own message seriously. People aren't stupid! They are watching how we run our churches, and so we need to make sure that our praise for our Creator is not just in the words we sing but in the lives we live."

"My heart is for the church, and my core focus is on the kingdom. I've seen how someone starting to engage and pray about this is changed from the inside out, and how it can widen the perspective of a church to so many other things. In that sense, creation care is the start, but not the end.

I'd like the church to really be heaven on earth. We have an interest in being salt and light that makes a difference to people's lives. That's why we need to demonstrate a care for creation at every level, from our local churches to praying over decision-making at the UN."

We cannot relegate creation care to our personal choices, though it will include those. Creation care is about how we, as part of our mission, seek to bring God's rule to creation: changing the way communities relate to God, to each other, and to the land. It inevitably implicates the complicated issues of land ownership and management, debt, social protection, and consumption.

The Anglican Consultative Council Resolution 17 says of the situation we face:

> This requires an active spiritual response: the church must urgently find its collective moral voice and become a living example of God's reconciled world.

In our response, we have to recognise that the difference between where we are and "God's reconciled world" is a massive one, and one which we can only bring about sustained by God-centred faith.

This call is reiterated by Swaziland Bishop Wamukoya in The World is Our Host - "We need to make our communities equal – as in the Eucharist. We consecrate enough but not more. Jesus died for all humanity equally." We do not take our equality before God seriously, and we see the outworking of this in the injustices of our carelessness, our greed and our exploitation of others. Restoring equality, becoming a living example of God's reconciled world, will help us end the injustices which are etched into landscapes, and which destabilise the climate.

The scale of the need and the crisis we face demands a commensurate change.

Injustice is so embedded into our way of life that 'urgent and prophetic ecological responsibility' will lead us to reimagine many things we consider to be either inevitable or unchangeable, and it will ask us to do the seemingly impossible.

> 'Urgent and prophetic ecological responsibility' will require change.

Our responsibility is urgent because our choices in the short-term have ramifications in the long-term. Our responsibility is prophetic because it asks us to return to the presence and call of God's covenant, and to not settle for anything other than the gospel, the reign of God in our own contexts.

Conclusion

In 2019, the year after I graduated university, I went to a report launch in London, and was witness to a moment that has stayed with me. An international climate lawyer emotionally described the fear that her work representing small island states at the UN climate change conferences had not been enough, and that her time working had gone to waste.

Another panellist turned to her, his voice full with emotion as he said,

"No time is wasted".

It was a rare moment of watching the professional veneer of a report launch crumble and be replaced with the rawness and vulnerability of love.

I'd like to suggest that our faith in the gospel tells us "no love is wasted".

The love of God, the redemption of Christ, and the transforming power of the Spirit, is the starting place for our mission. And it is love that begins, sustains and brings our mission to completion. Creation care derives from our response to the Creator, the Lordship of Jesus, and in this sense – when practised properly – it is no less than partnering with God in the reconciliation of all things.

> Mission is a work of loving reconciliation.

The mission of God in our fallen and broken world, accomplished in the work of Jesus Christ and entrusted to the church.

It takes place in the context of brokenness - between God and humanity, between humanity and the rest of creation and between people. The context of brokenness is also the context (and cause) of our environmental crises. Mission, our work of reconciliation in Christ, therefore has an integral environmental dimension.

This missional work of reconciliation takes place in our particular places and contexts; it therefore takes many different forms, as the examples in this booklet have shown. Doing this work in our own church, city, and country, and seeking to become "a living example of God's reconciled world" is difficult. Injustice is so embedded into our way of life that our mission will lead us to reimagine many things we consider to be either inevitable or unchangeable, and it will ask us to do the seemingly impossible.

And yet, no love is wasted.

> We serve a God of the impossible who takes our offerings and multiplies them.

And as we face the challenges before us, we remember that the most inevitable and unchangeable thing of this world is the certainty of death. And yet, that is precisely what faith in Christ leads us to deny.

As Christians we are called to bear witness to the love of God, which has overcome death. God's love for this world is greater than we dare imagine, and it is this love that begins, sustains and brings our mission to completion.

This is what integral mission and creation care is all about.

Bibliography and Further Reading

Atkinson, D., Climate Change and the Gospel (Operation Noah, 2015).

Bauckham, R., Bible and Ecology (TX: Baylor University Press, 2010).

Bookless, D., Planetwise: Dare to Care for God's World (Intervarsity Press, 2008).

Brown, E., Ruling God's World God's Way: Dominion in Psalm 8, in C.R. Bell, ed., Creation Care and the Gospel: Reconsidering the Mission of the Church (Hendrickson Publishers, 2016).

Brown, O., A. Hammill and R. McLeman, Climate change as the 'new' security threat: implications for Africa. (International Affairs 83.6, 2007).

Brueggemann, W., The Land: Place as Gift, Promise, and Challenge in Biblical Faith (Fortress Press, 2002).

Ceballos, G., et al., Biological annihilation via the ongoing sixth mass extinction signaled by vertebrate population losses and declines"(PNAS, 2017).

Christian Aid, The Climate of Poverty: Facts, Fears and Hope (Christian Aid, 2006).

Dirzo, R., et al., Defaunation in the Anthropocene (Science, 2014).

Gitau, S.K., The Environmental Crisis: A Challenge for African Christianity (2000).

Greene-McCreight, K., I Am With You: The Archbishop of Canterbury's Lent, (Bloomsbury Publishing, 2015)

Grooten, M., and R.E.A. Almond, eds., World Wide Fund for Nature Living Planet Report: Aiming Higher, (WWF, 2018)

Intergovernmental Panel on Climate Change, Special Report: Global Warming of 1.5°C (IPCC, 2018)

Kim, G., and H.P. Koster, eds., Planetary Solidarity: Global Women's Voices on Christian Doctrine and Climate Justice (Fortress Press, 2017).

Küng, H., On Being a Christian (Collins, 1977)

Lausanne Movement, The Cape Town Commitment, https://lausanne.org/content/ctcommitment, (Lausanne Movement, 2010)

Lausanne Movement, Creation Care and the Gospel: Jamaica Call to Action (Lausanne Movement, 2012)

Laybourn-Langton, L., L. Rankin and D. Baxter, "This is a crisis: Facing up to the age of environmental breakdown" (IPPR, 2019).

Makgoba, T., An interview with the Eco-bishops, Tearfund Footsteps Magazine 99 (Tearfund, 2016).

Micah Global, Micah Network Declaration on Integral Mission (Micah Network, 2001).

Millennium Ecosystem Assessment 2005. Ecosystems and human well-being: Synthesis, https://www.millenniumassessment.org/documents/ document.356.aspx.pdf (World Resources Institute, 2005).

Moo, J.A., A Biblical Basis for Creation Care, in C.R. Bell, ed., Creation Care and the Gospel: Reconsidering the Mission of the Church (Hendrickson Publishers, 2016).

Nakwatumbah, N., The World is our Host (ACEN, 2015).

Parks, R., et al., Experiences and lessons in managing water from Cape Town., Grantham Institute Briefing Paper, No.29 (Grantham Institute, 2019).

Sánchez-Bayo, F. and K. Wyckhuys, Worldwide decline of the entomofauna: A review of its drivers (Biological Conservation, vol 232, 2019).

Sharkey, S.A., Earth, Our Home: Biblical Witness in the Hebrew Scriptures (Sor Juana Press, 2004).

Sorley, C., Creation Care and the Great Commission, in Bell and White, eds., Creation Care and the Gospel (Hendrickson Press, 2016).

Stott, J., in Foreword to P. Harris, Under the Bright Wings (Regent College Publishing, 1993).

Stott, J., Issues Facing Christians Today (Zondervan, 1984).

Takayabu, I., et al., Climate change effects on the worst-case storm surge: A case study of Typhoon Haiyan. (Environmental Research Letters 10.6, 2015).

Vidal, J., Tip of the Iceberg: is our destruction of nature responsible for Covid-19? (The Guardian, 2020).

World Health Organization and Unicef, Progress on drinking water, sanitation and hygiene: 2017 update and SDG baselines. (World Health Organization, 2017).

Wright, C.J.H., God's People in God's Land: Family, Land and Property in the Old Testament, (Wm. B. Eerdmans Publishing, 2014).

Wright, C.J.H., The Mission of God: Unlocking the Bible's Grand Narrative (Inter-Varsity Press, 2013).

Wright, N.T., Relevant Magazine, July-August (Relevant Media Group, 2015).